DIY FOR BOYS

SPEED MACHINES

Go-kart

Rubber band
dragster

Customized
skateboard

by Ruth Owen

PowerKiDS
press

New York

Published in 2014 by The Rosen Publishing Group, Inc.
29 East 21st Street, New York, NY 10010

Produced for Rosen by Ruby Tuesday Books Ltd
Editor for Ruby Tuesday Books Ltd: Mark J. Sachner
US Editor: Joshua Shadowens
Designers: Tammy West and Emma Randall

With special thanks to Steve Owen for his help in developing and making
the projects in this book.

Photo Credits:
Cover, 1, 5, 6—7, 8—9, 10—11, 12—13, 14—15, 16—17, 18—19, 20—21,
22—23, 24—25, 26—27, 28—29 © Ruby Tuesday Books and John Such;
3, 4—5, 6—7, 10 © Shutterstock.

Library of Congress Cataloging-in-Publication Data

Owen, Ruth, 1967—
 Speed machines / Ruth Owen.
    pages cm. — (DIY for boys)
 Includes index.
 ISBN 978-1-4777-6274-5 (library binding) — ISBN 978-1-4777-6275-2 (pbk.) —
ISBN 978-1-4777-6276-9 (6-pack)
 1. Speed—Experiments—Juvenile literature. I. Title.
 QC137.52.O943 2014
 629.04'60228—dc23
                        2013035227

Manufactured in the United States of America

CPSIA Compliance Information: Batch #W14PK8 For Further Information contact: Rosen Publishing, New York, New York at 1-800-237-9932

CONTENTS

WARNING!

Neither the author nor the publisher shall be liable for any bodily harm or damage to property that may happen as a result of carrying out the projects in this book.

THE NEED FOR SPEED

If you love cars, racing, skateboarding, and all things fast and powerful, this is the book for you.

The day when you own your own car might still be a few years off, but in the meantime this book gives you a chance to be an **engineer**, an **auto mechanic**, and a driver by building a miniature **dragster** or a full-size **go-kart**.

If skateboarding's your thing, then this book will show you how to **customize** your deck and give it an incredible new look. And if you're fascinated by space travel, all you need is a soda bottle, some vinegar, and **baking soda** to go for launch and send a rocket blasting sky high!

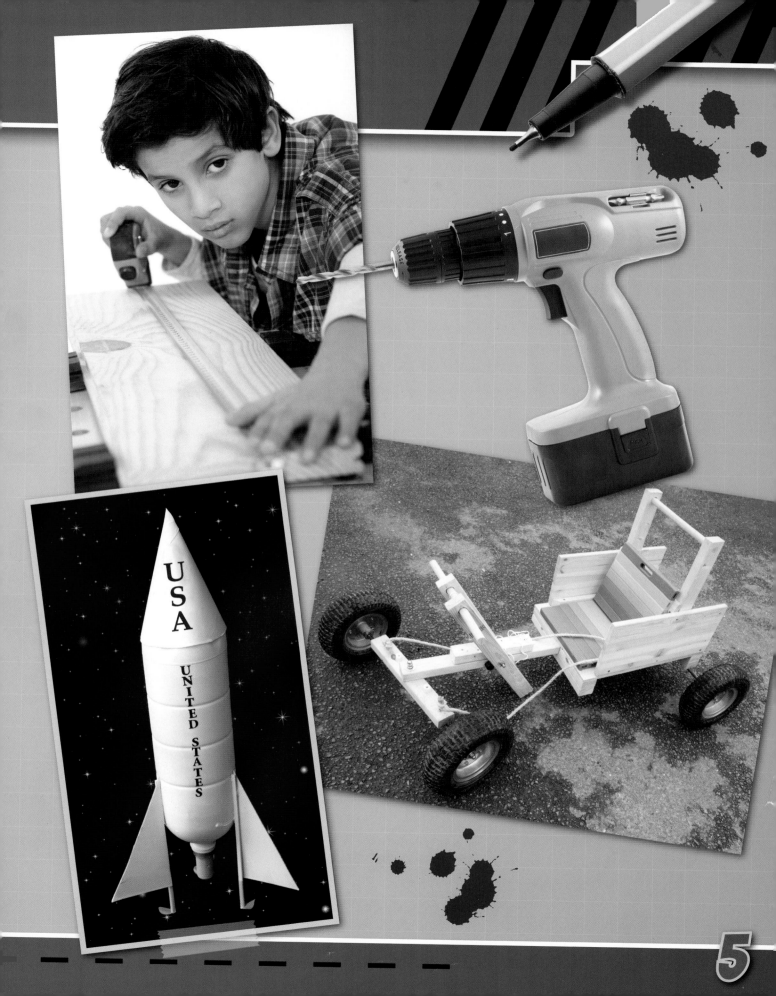

If your skateboard deck is looking old and battered, it's possible to give it a truly stylish and professional-looking new paint job. And the best thing is, you don't have to be artistic at all to create this effect!

All you will need to produce a fantastic design are some cans of spray paint and some dishwashing liquid. Do this project outside on a warm, sunny day so that the Sun helps the paint dry quickly. Also, it's best to work outside when using spray paint so that you are getting plenty of fresh air and not breathing in paint fumes.

Before

After

YOU WILL NEED:

- A skateboard
- Tools for removing the trucks
- Newspaper or a large piece of cardboard
- Cans of spray paint
- Dishwashing liquid
- Some water and a dishcloth
- A can of spray varnish

STEP 1:

You will need to buy white paint for a base coat, two or three colors of paint for the pattern, and a different color for the topcoat.

Spray paints that are used for fixing chips on cars and bikes are hard-wearing and come in a huge range of colors.

Black topcoat

Blue, purple, and pink pattern

STEP 2:

Remove the trucks from the skateboard.

STEP 3:

Place the deck on sheets of newspaper or a large piece of cardboard to protect the ground underneath. Spray the deck with white paint as a base coat. Allow the paint to dry.

STEP 4:

Now spray stripes or blocks of color on top of the white. Any pattern will do! Allow the paint to dry.

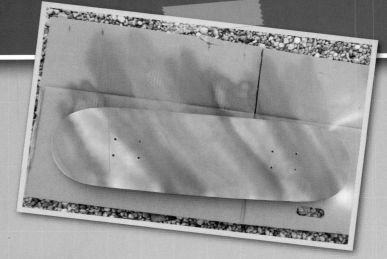

STEP 5:

Next, squirt dishwashing liquid over the deck in a swirly pattern.

Dishwashing liquid

STEP 6:

Allow the dishwashing liquid to dry for about 30 minutes. It won't get completely dry, but it will set, a little like jelly.

STEP 7:

Spray the whole deck with the topcoat color, covering all the other paint colors and the dishwashing liquid. Allow the paint to dry.

STEP 8:

When the topcoat is completely dry, moisten a dishcloth with water and gently start rubbing at the swirls made with dishwashing liquid. As you rub, the dishwashing liquid and any topcoat paint on the swirls will wash away, leaving a colorful pattern underneath.

STEP 9:

Allow the deck to dry. Cover the new paint job with spray varnish. Choose a brand that works with the kinds of spray paints you've used.

STEP 10:

When the varnish is completely dry, screw the trucks back on.

Here's an alternative color scheme you could try. Get creative!

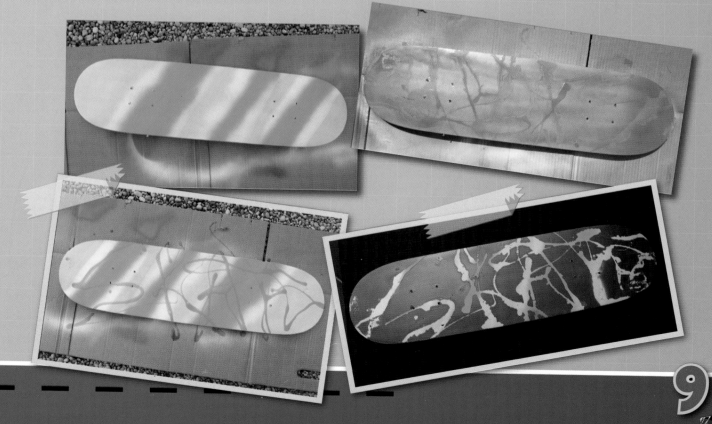

Drag racing is a motorsport in which high-speed, powerful cars or motorbikes race each other, usually two at a time.

Two dragsters race along a straight strip of track for a short distance, such as a quarter of a mile (400 m). The winner is the first to cross the finish line. Drag racing is exciting, fast, and very loud.

You'll have to make your own sound effects, but you can build your own miniature dragster that is powered by a rubber band. Get a friend involved, and each of you can build a dragster. Then line up your tiny speed machines and get racing!

A dragster

A rubber band dragster

YOU WILL NEED:
- 24 inches (61 cm) of plastic cable tubing
- A craft knife
- A small drill and an adult to help you use the drill
- 14 inches (36 cm) of wooden doweling, about the thickness of a pencil, for the axles
- 8 inches (20 cm) of wooden doweling, thinner than a pencil, for the stability struts
- 4 plastic milk bottle tops
- 2 small plastic lids
- 2 push pins
- 2 plastic soda bottle tops
- 2 CDs
- A glue gun
- A wooden skewer
- A long rubber band, or several rubber bands tied together
- A section of old electrical cable. You need the outer casing.

STEP 1:

Cut two sections of plastic cable tubing 12 inches (30.5 cm) long. These are the sides of the dragster.

Ask an adult to drill a hole all the way through the tubing at both ends. The four holes should be a snug fit for the pieces of doweling you will use for the axles.

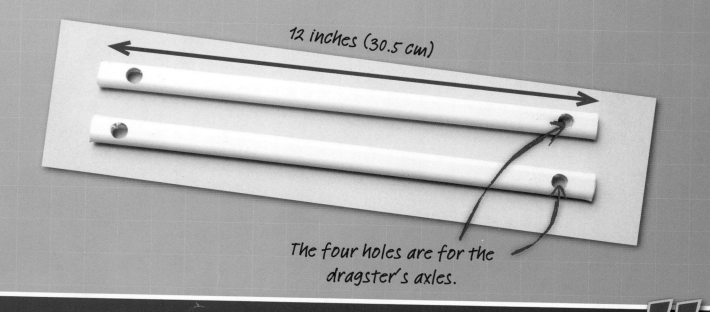

12 inches (30.5 cm)

The four holes are for the dragster's axles.

STEP 2:

Ask an adult to drill four more holes. These holes should be inside the axle holes and only through one side of the tubing. The four holes must be a snug fit for the stability struts.

Holes for stability struts

STEP 3:

Cut the thinner doweling into two 4-inch- (10-cm-) long pieces. Then push these pieces into the four inner holes to make the dragster's stability struts.

Stability struts

The struts will keep the dragster's frame rigid.

This hole should be a snug fit for the axle.

STEP 4:

To make each front wheel, you will need a plastic milk bottle top, a small, circular plastic lid, and a push pin. Ask an adult to drill a hole (the size of the axle) into each bottle top.

STEP 5:
To assemble the front wheels, cut a 6-inch- (15-cm-) long section of the thicker doweling. Thread this through the front axle holes.

Front axle

STEP 6:
Thread a milk bottle top onto the axle. Place the lid against the bottle top and press the push pin through the lid into the end of the axle. Repeat on the other side.

STEP 7:
To make each rear wheel, you will need a milk bottle top, a soda bottle top, and a CD.

STEP 8:
Glue the soda bottle top into the exact center of the CD.

WARNING:
Only use a glue gun if an adult is there to help you.

STEP 9:
Turn the CD over and glue the milk bottle top to the exact center of the CD.

STEP 10:

To assemble the rear wheels, you will need the remaining 8-inch (20-cm) section of the thicker doweling.

STEP 11:

Ask an adult to drill a hole in the milk bottle top that's glued to the CD. The hole should be a snug fit for the back axle. Thread the axle through the bottle tops and CD. To hold the axle in place, squeeze some glue around the axle where it enters the hole.

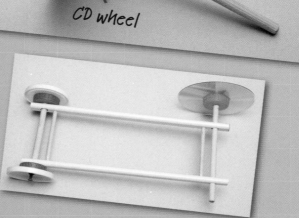

Soda bottle top hubcap

Squeeze glue around here

Back axle

CD wheel

STEP 12:

Thread the rear axle through the rear axle holes. Then assemble and attach the second rear wheel.

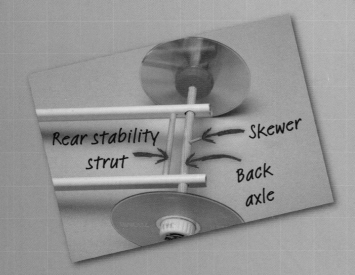

Rear stability strut

Skewer

Back axle

STEP 13:

Ask an adult to drill a small hole about halfway through the rear axle. The hole should be a snug fit for a wooden skewer. Put some glue on a short length of wooden skewer, then press the skewer into the hole. Trim the skewer so that when the rear axle turns, the skewer doesn't touch the rear stability strut.

STEP 14:

If you wish, you can make tires from the plastic outer casing of electrical cable. Glue or tape the tires in place before assembling the wheels. You can also paint the wheels.

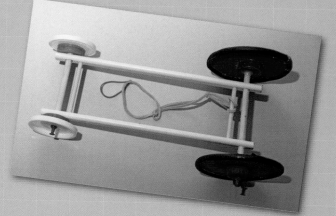

STEP 15:

To get the dragster running, take a long rubber band, or several bands tied together. Securely loop the rubber band around the rear stability strut.

STEP 16:

Stretch the rubber band around the front stability strut, pull it back to the rear axle, and hook it over the skewer.

STEP 17:

Turn the rear wheels and axle backward so that the rubber band winds around the rear axle as many times as possible. Keep hold of the rear wheels.

When you are ready for the dragster to race, let go of the rear wheels. The rubber band will quickly unwind, turning the back axle, and powering the dragster forward. Super fast!

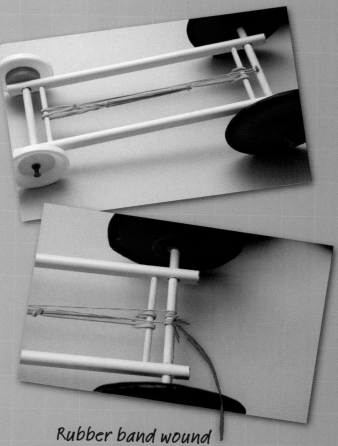

Rubber band wound around rear axle

The key ingredients for making a go-kart are the wheels and **axles**. They might come from an old baby carriage or stroller, or you might use wheels from old wheelbarrows or carts.

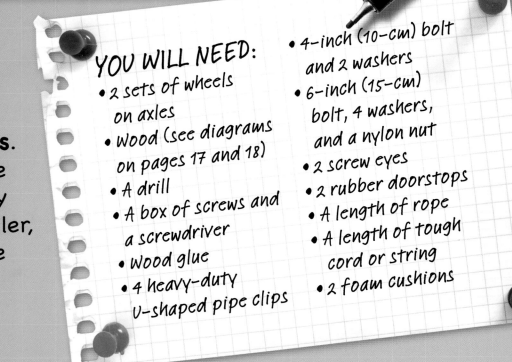

YOU WILL NEED:
- 2 sets of wheels on axles
- Wood (see diagrams on pages 17 and 18)
- A drill
- A box of screws and a screwdriver
- Wood glue
- 4 heavy-duty U-shaped pipe clips
- 4-inch (10-cm) bolt and 2 washers
- 6-inch (15-cm) bolt, 4 washers, and a nylon nut
- 2 screw eyes
- 2 rubber doorstops
- A length of rope
- A length of tough cord or string
- 2 foam cushions

Once you've found your wheels and axles, all you need to do is follow our plan, customizing the sizes of the wooden parts to suit your wheels and axles. To make the go-kart, you'll need to use a drill, so get an adult on board to assist you, and have fun building this project as a team!

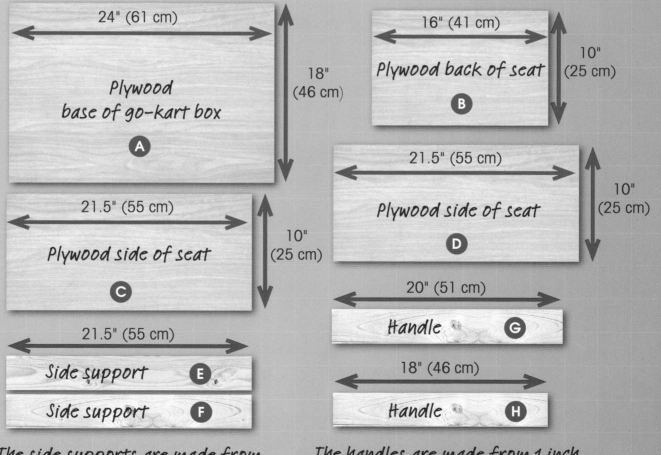
24 inches (61 cm)

STEP 1:

First find your wheels. Our wheels came from an old cart, the kind used at a garden center to carry plants. The axles were 24 inches (61 cm) long. All of the wooden parts were made to fit these axles.

STEP 2:

The wooden parts you will need to make the go-kart are shown below and on page 18. They are named and labeled with the letters of the alphabet.

24" (61 cm)

18" (46 cm)

Plywood
base of go-kart box

A

16" (41 cm)

10" (25 cm)

Plywood back of seat

B

21.5" (55 cm)

10" (25 cm)

Plywood side of seat

C

21.5" (55 cm)

10" (25 cm)

Plywood side of seat

D

20" (51 cm)

Handle

G

21.5" (55 cm)

Side support

E

18" (46 cm)

Handle

H

Side support

F

The side supports are made from pieces of 2 x 1 inch (5 x 2.5 cm) wood

The handles are made from 1 inch (2.5 cm) thick doweling

The following parts are all made from wood that measures 2.5 x 1.5 inches (6 x 4 cm).

48" (122 cm)

Spine **I**

18" (46 cm)

Front axle **J**

Rear axle **K**

Center support **L**

8" (20 cm)

M   **N**

O   **P**

Support blocks

20" (51 cm)

Push handle **Q**

Push handle **R**

24" (61 cm)

Brake **S**

Brake **T**

12" (30.5 cm)

Brake **U**

STEP 3:
Take the wooden front axle (part J) and drill a hole through the center. Thread a 4-inch (10-cm) bolt through the hole.

Bolt

STEP 4:
Attach part J to the front axle of the wheels. Use heavy-duty, U-shaped pipe clips to screw part J to the axle.

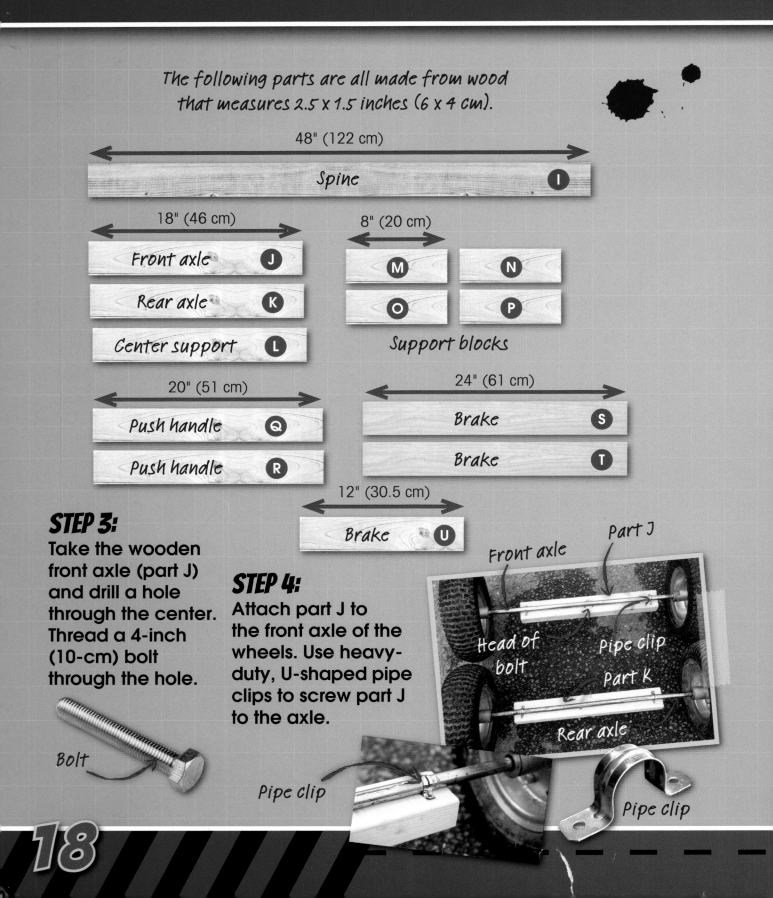

Front axle

Part J

Head of bolt

Pipe clip

Part K

Rear axle

Pipe clip

Pipe clip

STEP 5:

Using pipe clips, screw the wooden rear axle (part K) to the rear axle of the wheels.

STEP 6:

Drill a hole in one end of the spine (part I). Then attach the spine to the front axle (part J) as follows:

Place a washer over the bolt in part J.

Bolt

Part J

Washer

Cap nut

Spine (Part I)

Part J

Slot part I over the bolt. Add another washer. Screw a cap nut in place.

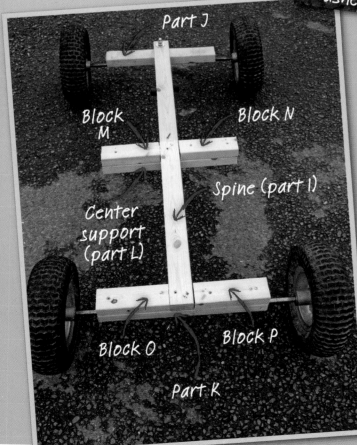

Part J

Block M

Block N

Spine (part I)

Center support (part L)

Block O

Block P

Part K

STEP 7:

Screw the rear end of the spine (part I) to the rear axle (part K).

STEP 8:

Screw the center support (part L) under the spine so that it is 24 inches (61 cm) from the rear end of the spine.

STEP 9:

Screw the support blocks M and N to the top of part L.

STEP 10:

Screw the support blocks O and P to the top of part K.

STEP 11:

Drill a narrow hole 2 inches (5 cm) from each end of the front axle (part J). Insert a screw eye into each hole and screw in tightly.

STEP 12:

To stop the front wheels from locking, screw a rubber doorstop to the front axle (part J) on each side of the spine (part I). Each doorstop should be 4 inches (10 cm) from the spine.

STEP 13:

Tie a loop of rope to the screw eyes. The go-kart's driver will use this rope for steering the front wheels.

Front axle (part J)

Doorstops

A screw eye with rope handle threaded through

Screw eye

Screw the base here

STEP 14:

Screw the base of the go-kart's box, or seat, (part A) to the spine (part I) and to blocks M, N, O, and P.

Base (part A)

Screw the base here

STEP 15:

To assemble the sides of the box, or seat, stand one side (part C) on the edge of the base (part A). Place a side support (part E) against C. Screw part E into the base. Then, from the outside, screw part C to part E.

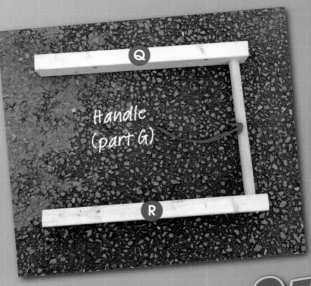

Side of seat (part C)

Side support (part E)

Base (part A)

STEP 16:

Repeat step 15 on the other side of the box by screwing a side support (part F) into the base. Then screw side of seat (part D) to part F.

STEP 17:

To make the push handle, drill a 1-inch (2.5-cm) hole in the end of parts Q and R.

STEP 18:

Insert the handle (part G) into the holes in parts Q and R so it is flush with the outer sides of Q and R. Glue and screw part G in place.

Handle (part G)

STEP 19:

Position the push handle about halfway into the box. Screw the push handle parts Q and R to the sides of the box parts C and D.

STEP 20:

Place the seat back (part B) into the box and screw to parts Q and R.

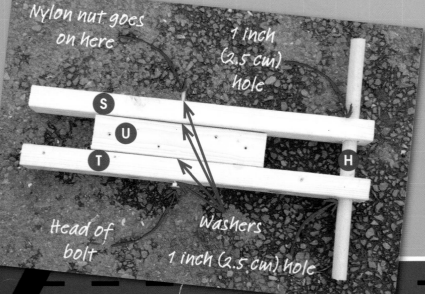

Push handle (part G)

R

Seat back (part B)

Q

C

D

STEP 21:

Finally, to make the go-kart's brake, drill a 1-inch (2.5-cm) hole in one end of part S and part T.

STEP 22:

Next, measure 10 inches (25 cm) from the other end of parts S and T and drill a hole through the center of each part large enough for the 6-inch (15-cm) bolt. Also, drill the same-sized hole through the center of part U.

STEP 23:

Join parts S, T, and U together by threading a 6-inch (15-cm) bolt through the holes you drilled. You must put a washer between the head of the bolt and the wood, between each piece of wood, and over the bolt before securing the bolt with a nylon nut.

STEP 24:

Slide the handle (part H) through the 1-inch (2.5-cm) holes in parts S and T. Glue and screw the handle in place.

Nylon nut goes on here

1 inch (2.5 cm) hole

S

U

T

H

Head of bolt

Washers

1 inch (2.5 cm) hole

STEP 25:

Using four screws, screw part U to the spine (part I).

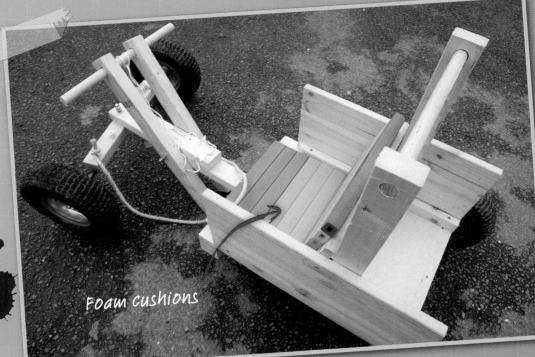

STEP 26:

Tie a piece of cord around the brake's handle (part H). To stop the go-kart, the driver pulls the cord and pulls part H toward him or her. Parts S and T will then make contact with the ground and stop the go-kart.

Foam cushions

Your go-kart is ready to go!

BLAST-OFF ROCKET

This project shows you how to build a plastic bottle rocket that's powered by vinegar and baking soda. Please don't try to launch your rocket indoors, though. This speed machine is strictly for outdoor use only!

STEP 1:
Glue the lengths of wood to the side of the soda bottle. They must be evenly spaced apart and all glued at exactly the same level so that the bottle can stand on them like legs.

STEP 2:
Pour the vinegar into the bottle.

Legs

White vinegar

A plastic wrap and baking soda sausage

STEP 3:
Place the baking soda onto a square of plastic wrap. Then wrap the baking soda to form a sausage shape that will fit into the neck of the bottle.

WARNING:
Only use a glue gun if an adult is there to help you.

YOU WILL NEED:

- An empty 2-liter soda bottle
- 3 pieces of thin doweling wood 7 inches (18 cm) long
- A craft knife
- A glue gun
- 2 pints (1 l) white vinegar
- 2 tablespoons of baking soda
- Plastic wrap
- A cork that's the right size to seal the neck of the soda bottle

STEP 4:

Take the rocket outside. Put the baking soda sausage into the bottle. Press in the cork. Turn the bottle (or rocket) upside-down, and stand well back.

A chemical reaction will cause pressure to build inside the rocket until it blasts the cork from the bottle sending the rocket skyward!

STEP 5:

Why not try a few practice launches to get your technique perfect? Then decorate a rocket and invite some friends to a launch.

5 4 3 2 1 . . . BLAST OFF!

A party hat nose cone

USA
UNITED STATES

White paint

Stick-on lettering

Straws

Cardboard fins

25

POPSICLE STICK RAFT

Using just wooden popsicle sticks, a glue gun, and a craft knife, you can build a **raft** that will actually move across water powered only by a rubber band.

When your miniature raft is ready, you can either launch it in a bathtub of water or take it to a pond or swimming pool for its **maiden voyage**. Be warned, this little raft is small, but it can really move!

WARNING:

Only use a glue gun if an adult is there to help you.

STEP 1:

Place about 10 or 11 popsicle sticks next to each other to create a square. This is the body of the raft. The top and bottom edges of the square should be the length of one popsicle stick.

This side should be as long as one stick.

YOU WILL NEED:

• Popsicle sticks
• A craft knife
• A glue gun
• A rubber band

STEP 2:

Next, you will need to glue one popsicle stick across the raft. This stick should be spaced down from the top of the square. Use one stick, as shown, to measure the distance from the top of the square, and then glue the second stick in place beneath it.

STEP 3:

Repeat Step 2 at the bottom of the square. Then glue a popsicle stick across the center of the raft.

Use one stick as a measure.

Glue this stick in place.

STEP 4:

Now glue one stick at the top of the square and one at the bottom, as shown.

STEP 5:

Turn the raft over, and glue one stick at the top of the square and one at the bottom, as shown. These two sticks should be in line with the two sticks glued on in Step 4.

STEP 6:

When all the glue has dried, stretch a rubber band across the two pairs of sticks.

STEP 7:

Now, to make the paddle that drives the raft, cut four 2-inch- (5-cm-) long pieces of popsicle stick.

2 inches (5 cm)

STEP 8:

Now, cut four more pieces of popsicle stick. Glue two pieces to the paddle as shown. The gap between the two pieces should be the width of the rubber band.

STEP 9:

Turn the paddle over, and glue the remaining two pieces of popsicle stick to the other side so that they line up with the first pair.

Glue these two popsicle sticks.

This gap is the width of the rubber band

STEP 10:
Trim off any ends of popsicle stick to create a square.

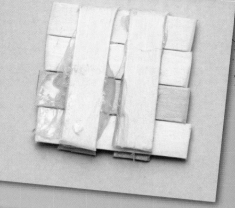

STEP 11:
When all the glue has dried, place the paddle so that the rubber band sits in the gaps between the popsicle sticks.

STEP 12:
The raft is now ready to go. If you wish, you can decorate it. We've used a pirate cupcake flag!

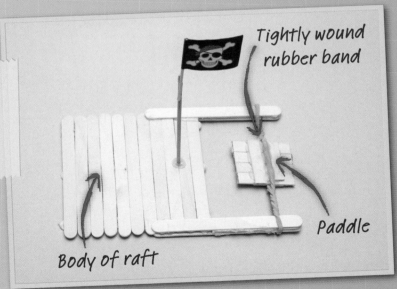

Tightly wound rubber band

Paddle

Body of raft

STEP 13:
To make the raft move across water, twist or wind the paddle backward away from the body of the raft so that the rubber band is twisted around many times.

STEP 14:
Holding the tightly wound paddle in place, lower the raft into a bathtub of water or onto a pond or swimming pool. Let go of the paddle. As the rubber band unwinds, the paddle will drive the raft through the water!

auto mechanic (AW-toh mih-KA-nik)
A skilled person who is trained to make repairs or alterations to a car. A mechanic may work in a garage or may sometimes be part of the team that builds or repairs a racing car.

baking soda (BAYK-ing SOH-duh)
A white powder that is known scientifically as sodium bicarbonate. It has many uses, but it is often used in the cooking of bread and other baked goods as an ingredient to make the baked item expand so its texture is lighter and fluffier.

customize (KUS-tuh-myz)
To alter something to your own specifications, especially in order to make it unusual or unique.

drag racing (DRAG RAY-sing)
A high-speed race on a short, straight track usually between two cars, known as dragsters, or two motorbikes. Drag races test how fast a vehicle can accelerate from a standing start. The first vehicle to cross the finish line is the winner.

dragster (DRAG-stur)
A car that has been specially built or customized to take part in drag races.

engineer (en-juh-NEER)
A skilled person who uses math, science, and technology to design and build machines such as cars or spacecraft, or structures such as bridges or skyscrapers.

go-kart (GOH-kart)
A small vehicle that is low to the ground and usually has four wheels. Go-karts may be fitted with engines or powered by one person pushing the vehicle to get it moving while another rides and steers.

maiden voyage (MAY-den VOY-ij)
The first official voyage, or journey, of a watercraft such as a boat or ship.

raft (RAFT)
A simple flat boat made by tying, or fixing, together a number of logs, planks of wood, or other materials that will float.

WEBSITES

Due to the changing nature of Internet links, Powerkids Press has developed an online list of websites related to the subject of this book. This site is updated regularly. Please use this link to access the list:
www.powerkidslinks.com/dfb/speed/

READ MORE

Georgiou, Tyrone. *Top Fuel Dragsters.* Fast Lane: Drag Racing. New York: Gareth Stevens, 2011.

Gross, Miriam. *All About Rockets.* Blast Off! New York: PowerKids Press, 2009.

Sohn, Emily. *Skateboarding: How It Works.* The Science of Sports. Mankato, MN: Capstone Press, 2010.

INDEX